THE MAGIC OF MOMENTS

From Mindfulness to Reflection

ALSO BY JOAN KANTOR

Shadow Sounds

Fading Into Focus

Holding It Together

Too Close For Comfort

THE MAGIC OF MOMENTS

From Mindfulness to Reflection

Poems *on* Nature

JOAN KANTOR

ISBN-13: 978-0692667309
ISBN-10: 069266730X
LCCN: 2016936357
WovenWord Press, Canton CT

Dedication

I would like to thank my husband, Chuck, for the enormous amount of support and patience he has shown throughout my writing life and for his incredible technical support. I would also like to thank my friends, Cheryl Golfin and June Barta, for their excellent and honest feedback, and Nan Runde for the generous use of her beautifully rendered and ethereal drawings. As always, I want to thank my friend and mentor, Rennie McQuilkin, for helping me grow as a writer. Mostly, I want to thank my father for introducing me to the magical world of nature.

Acknowledgements

In Between------------------------The Avocet
A Hint-----------------------------The Avocet
Blur Of Colors---------------------The Avocet
Centered---------------------------The Avocet
The Nature of Ecstasy--------------The Avocet
On The Cusp-----------------------The Avocet
Agnostic---------------------------Birmingham Journal of the Arts
Holiday Decorations---------------Word Art
Unaware---------------------------Word Art
Control----------------------------Fresh Ink
Seduction--------------------------Autumn Sky Poetry Daily
Daylight Savings-----------------Autumn Sky Poetry Daily

Lullaby----------------------------Inlandia
Power------------------------------Inlandia
Why They Fish-------------------Caduceus
In Between------------------------Your Daily Poem

Table of Contents

Introduction

In the Deep

In The Swim / 33

Beyond Bare Branches

Winterlude

Saving The Seasons

About the Author

"This silence, this moment, every moment, if it's genuinely inside you, brings what you need."

~ Rumi

Introduction

I've been writing nature poems for as long as I can remember, and finally decided to devote an entire collection to them. Being in nature is transformative for me; it instantly brings me to a place of peaceful joy, creativity and contemplation. Many of these poems' first drafts were actually written out in nature, and almost all of those that are water-related were first written while I was either in or on the water, my favorite place to be. I often feel more at home in the water than on land. You'll notice that there are numerous poems related to this passion for water as well as my fascination with geese, Queen Anne's Lace and fiddlehead ferns; the latter two seemingly so human. There are fewer poems about autumn and winter. Only recently did I come to fully appreciate fall's beauty, since I used to foolishly spend my time mourning the loss of swimming. I adore winter, but sadly the cold often keeps me indoors and at a distance from those up-close experiences that inspire my writing.

Over the years, this city girl has come to appreciate the magical qualities of even the briefest moments in nature. I've learned to be a good observer and to notice the not so obvious. Some of my most amazing experiences outdoors have happened in just a matter of seconds or minutes. You will find that there are more than a few equally brief poems. I'm a very visual person, and some of these poems are what I like to refer to as "word snapshots" or "word paintings".

The natural world is often a vehicle for me to calmly look deeper, see connections and the juxtaposition of harshness and beauty, life and death. It fills me with a sense of spirituality and brings me to a place of heightened awareness; a meditative state that is both conscious and subconscious. Often, I experience a stillness that very gradually populates itself with images, words and reflections. In this slowed down quiet state, I am able to receive gifts whose meanings I may not fully understand, yet trust are there. Often after rereading one of my nature-inspired poems, I discover a metaphor or see ties to things I didn't realize I was connecting, though there was clearly an inner intention to do so. I love the rush of becoming one with something so magnificent that also parallels human existence. I take equal joy in finding later that what I experienced and then crafted into words, is different or even deeper than I thought at the time.

In this high pressure digital world, it's easy to lose sight of the beauty before us. If you take a little time out of your busy schedule to notice nature, you too might discover the magic of moments in a peaceful place of mindful reflection.

Nature Is A Way Into Ourselves

In The Deep

Swimming
I whisper words
over ripples and waves
and breathe them back in
where they stay

till I place them on paper

Later
rereading my poem
I suddenly see
the metaphors
I wrote the day before
and realize
I'm in deeper
than I thought

Emergence

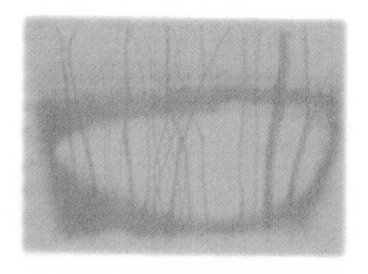

"Be like a flower and turn your face to the sun."

~ Kahlil Gibran

Invasion

Finding invisible fissures in rock,
poking through layers
of pine needle sponge
and mounds of brittle beige leaves

unstoppable

it's even popped up
in murky brown puddles

this welcome invasion
of green

Sleight of Hand

You disappeared
into steamy swirls
of last summer's heat

Now suddenly,
with springtime's flow
you've returned

a vernal pool
tinted with tannin
from autumn's leaves

You suddenly fill
with the promise
of egg-sacks adrift
and tadpoles
        wriggling
    their tails

But along
    with the magic
            of tadpoles
  turning into frogs

with a snap
        of summer's
                scalding fingers

you'll be gone

Incipient

I open my windows
to the scent
of rising sap
and thaw.
the hazy sight
of yellow-green buds
on almost bare branches,
and the clatter
of construction crews.

Though the grass remains beige
the sky
cool and grey,
still the warmth
of scattered crocuses
poking up
purple and pink,
is shifting
the seasons
into gear.

Making Room

Determined
delicate beech leaves
clinging to trees
through winter
and into spring

translucent
wizened-white
parchment-like
in the breeze
quiver
with crinkling sounds

Soon
bright green
newborn ones
will push
these elders out

As If

they knew
        my hopes
                they flew
                        so close
                                in their jagged
                                        dark brown V
                                                that I could see
                                                their black
                                tucked-under feet
                        and hear the delicate
                whizzing sound
of flapping wings

Magic Cabbages

Inspired by the early spring skunk cabbage beside the river in Canton, CT

Their roots forever reach deep
in the wet
while pushing up delicate spears
that soon will be burgundy swirls
yellow-flecked
whose outspreading oversized leaves
as they morph into green
will unfold
in a spiral
of fans

Jonquil

From atop a bright green stem
            she toots her own horn
                      bellowing yellow and white
Surpassing the monotone daffodil
                  her trumpet plays two brilliant tones

Waiting Their Turn

At the edge of the woods,
between river and field,
surrounded by swirling skunk-cabbage leaves,
brilliant dandelion bursts
and lanky brown weeds with cream-colored fringe,
these fiddlehead ferns,
sprouting tall in the dirt,
so ready but yet to unfurl

are waiting their turn

and there's tension
in the taut anticipation
of upright chartreuse spines,
curved bent-over necks
and tightly curled heads
pressed into chests

yet
with an imperceptible quiver,
they still continue to tuck themselves in,
stay hidden,
eyes closed

till finally
       sunshine tells them
                   it's time to unfold.

Dance Of The Ferns

In their first performance
in the corps de ballet,
these yellow-green
freshly born ferns
unfurl.
En pointe
stretching tall,
they curve upwards,
in perfect alignment,
heads tilted back,
arms reaching out,
fingers fluttering
feathery fronds,
as synchronized,
they sway
in the breeze.

In Spite Of

Though incipient spring
still blows brittle and cold
the trees are aglow
in a haze of yellow-green
Dogwood blossoms
are upwardly swelling
in burgundy blending to pink
Forsythia is exploding
in wild-popcorn-profusion
of bright-yellow petals and buds
   as cherry trees
       draping their arms
            joyfully weep
                purple tears

Oxymoron

Little brown bird
feather-fur fluff
in a lump
at my feet

you've met
the end
at the beginning

April Fools

Yawning and stretching
        budding thawed trees
                awakening to the sun
are caught in a storm
        of squalling ice wind
and suddenly
                swaddled
                        in white

Witness

Great Pond, Simsbury, CT

So calm beyond
    the mating dance
of honks
    and flapping wings

The sated geese
      glide on the pond
 energy
    all spent

Knowing
   they have just performed
their eyes
    confide
       in me

In Need of a Weed

Disheveled
with roots
firmly stuck
in dirt

your free-spirit's
spiky
and oddly shaped leaves
point every which way

so out of place

next to
a symmetrical border
of blossoms

Why is it *you*
almost everyone
wishes
were gone

The Find

Sessions Woods, Burlington, CT

There's a sign
on busy Route 69,
just a name
not a place
till today

Following Beaver Pond Trail
past birthing skunk cabbage,
unfurling huge ribbons
of yellow-green leaves by the stream
in the shadow of trees,
walking up and down hills
past meadow and woods,
finding swamp and beaver pond
spiked with dead trees,
lilies afloat,
green buds beneath water
so clear,
tinted brown,
moving on from Monet,
never dreaming
there could be more

a Japanese vision appears

a sheer veil of water
glistening
falls from above
onto mossy green rocks
filling pools,
spilling over
and into
my world.

Germination

Seed pearls
    sewn
        on feathery veils
release themselves
          to the wind
      where swinging
             and swaying
     in a downward drift
         they scatter themselves
        upon earth

Afterscent

Inland hurricane, Carbondale, IL, May 2009*

In the land of tornados
you surprised us all

miles wide,
your wild winds spinning round

roaring, ripping
and pulling the world apart

uprooting trees onto homes,
overturning trucks,
tossing live wires
onto lawns,
into streets

then suddenly still

For hours afterward,
the smell of raw green earthy guts,
torn trees, leaves, acidity
filled the air,
till the acrid smoke
from charcoal grills
wafting everywhere
overtook the silent scent
of fear.

*An inland hurricane is a rare meteorological event.

Disappearing Act

Perfectly round
and rainbow reflective,
the shiny black surface
of this tiny cabochon*
shimmers indigo
emerald,
purple,
gold

a delicate jewel
to grace
an elegant pinky finger

but instead,
it rests
on the sun-warmed curve
of a leaf

till suddenly
its brilliance
breaks open

as wings lift
        in silent flight,
    instantly
            melding miniscule
                        with sky

*A cabochon is a gemstone without facets that is round on top and flat on the
bottom.

Parenting Styles

Beside the school, tennis courts and track,
on a sandy pile of construction debris,
this enormous mother turtle's on a mission,
doesn't care where her eggs seem to endlessly fall,
dozens of rubbery-white shiny-wet ovals.

When done, she digs and covers them all,
then lumbering, hauls herself off
and I doubt she'll be there when they hatch.
Still most will survive on their own
and though I question her instinct of benign neglect,
there's a hint of envy within me
as I wonder if it even makes a difference.

Water Song I

Water's the tunesmith
        of melody motion
    humming
            its ripples
                and swirls
        in a dance
            over stones
                slipping
                    and sliding
                            soothingly
                    strumming
            the shore

Awakening I

Though your bright green body
is curled up tight
in a fuzzy blanket of tan
  when the sun shines down
      you'll slowly unfurl
         to soak up the warmth
            with your fronds

Agnostic

As I pass
by a patch
of greyish-green plants

my eye catches
the morning light
reflecting
from a leftover drop
of dew

whose translucent tension
lets the color
show through

It's impossible
how she holds together
the quivering
taut bulge
of herself

doesn't drip
or slide
down a stem

but clings
to the drooping
curved edge
of a leaf

tempting me

with belief

Fear

New York Botanical Gardens

She stands apart
from the rest of the plants
who opening up
reach out
to greet Spring

Though lithe
and tall
she arches forward
into herself
and tightly curled
her upper body
forms a fuzzy
reddish-tan coil

She's forgotten there's sunlight
and bright yellow-green

This fiddlehead
will never
unfurl

Integration

There's a letting loose
    in the sudden passion
        of a wind rippled puddle
     where cultivated flowers
       joyfully
         merge
          their reflections
      with those
    of lanky gold weeds
swinging and swaying
     in a colorful dance
        of mauve
      amber
    shadow and light
on a liquid floor
  of purple
    green
  pink
    in the mingling magic
        of them all

Different Dances

The orchid
sitting on my sill
with its subtle flare
petite and perfectly formed flat petals
painted with delicate dots of magenta
on a background
of green-tinged white
languidly bends her body
in a slow-motion waltz
that will last
for months

Outside my window
an exuberant iris
rises high above the garden
and everything about her shouts flashy

Propelled
by her long-leafed arms
her flowers explode
from the top of a tall and sturdy green stem
but they won't last long
and trying to get our attention
she stomps her heels
rhythmically clicks her castanets
and with her spine stretched taut
head tossed back
flaunting her wild flamenco ruffles
of deep purple and mauve
with inner hints
of bright white and gold
she knows her dance must be bold

Late May Meditation

Full of the season's
welcoming warmth
I barely feel
the bitter chill
as I slip beneath the surface
back into my watery world

I close my eyes
and bobbing
slosh
to the mantra
of gentle waves
sensing the ripples of fish
beneath my dangling feet
and surrounded
by the raw scent
of earth
I float
in the glimmering
darkness
of lake

Seeing Beneath the Surface

In the beaver pond,
with its burnished brown-green
waxy leaves of lilies

and their spiky blossoms
of yellow/pink/white

two spotlit
spotted fish

in murky tan water,
amidst specks
of sparkling silt

are almost unseen,
as shimmying
they swim
beneath the surface

Misty Meditation

*a cool Spring morning at Hammonasset Beach
State Park, Madison CT*

A distant fog horn
        deeply purrs
                its velvet mantra
as the undulating
             slow-motion surface
                          of The Sound
           alternates slick dark shadows
      with shimmers of silvery light
while rolling
        its gentle ripples
                toward shore
where they slosh
        against a sandy beige canvas
of finely crushed
      shells and stone
           forming lacy patches of foam
                        beneath
                  an infinite
             hazy grey
          softness

Worth The Wait

The late spring 1979 "17 Year Cicada* hatching",
Long Island, NY

It's time to wake up
  after seventeen years
    to unearth yourselves
      pull back your blankets of soil
        and emerge by the hundreds
     and hundreds of thousands
    to shed your shells
      fly high and full of life
        overwhelming the world
          with the magnitude
            of your mating songs
              and in a three week
                crescendo
              of revelry
         burn yourselves out
     leaving behind
    millions of eggs
     and emptied-out husks
      of happiness
        clinging to trees

Misnomer

"Nature likes to hide itself." ~ Heraclitus

From slimy brown molting nymph
your rainbow rotors rise newborn
from water plants and muck
to conjure up false cues
of stingers
stuck in tender flesh

Like whirring helicopter blades
your buzzing wings
make people cringe
from violet-emerald hues

till lightly you descend
upon a nearby leaf
and silently
Tiffany translucence
lacy-veined
reminds us
that all dragonflies
are damsels*

* Both dragonflies and damselflies belong to the order Odonata.

Before The Picnic

A hazy blanket
    of budding chartreuse
   is flavoring air
      with green,
    spreading the table
        for summer

In The Swim

"In summer, the song sings itself."

~ *William Carlos Williams*

"A lake carries you into recesses of feeling
otherwise impenetrable."

~ *William Wadsworth*

Centered

The labyrinth at Wisdom House, Litchfield, CT

It's early afternoon
in the midst of a heat wave
and though the air is stifling,
the sun's blinding brilliance
is beginning to sear my skin
and I probably should wait until evening,
while looking ahead
toward the labyrinth below
I remove my sandals,
press my feet into the grass,
crisp yet still slightly spongy-cool
from the rain-soaked soil
of last night's storm.
I pretend I'm a river
   flowing down the slope
and when I reach the bottom
I gaze
 at distant hills
   through a gap in the trees,
listen and watch
 delicate birch leaves
flash silver and green
 as they rustle and rattle
in a dance with warm air,
then I walk
   the puzzle of circular paths,
slowly wend my way to the center,
   and with soft rhythmic breaths
 I stand perfectly still,
 full
of purpose and peace.

Disguised

I follow this ritual path
through summer
to salt marsh

Each year
shedding my shell
expanding
I grow a new one

The Horseshoe Crab
disguises
its spidery roots

I too
am not what I seem

Leaving Sadness Behind

I float
to the mingled scent
of pine
water
grass and soil
as I stare at clouds
drifting in azure

From the corner of my eye
I glimpse the still brilliant sun
as it sinks
into a swaying green fringe

Weightless
I lie
in liquid silk
and total silence

that gently I break
into tinkling ripples
with outspreading arms

then with lids at half-mast
I gaze
through a shimmer of lash
and tiny droplets of prism

at turquoise-orange
silver-cobalt and gold
kaleidoscope flashes
of joy

Why They Fish

Farmington River, Riverton, CT

While rounding
      the bend,
   breathless
we're struck
    by a summer evening surprise
      of floating mist
         hugging the river
   as fly-fishermen,
      waist high in water,
    fishing
  in a trance,
gently
   whip
     their bright orange lines
       in a slow-motion dance
I'm sure
they've forgotten
their wish.

Lost in the Lake

I stand
beyond waist deep in water
as my feet
encountering autumn's debris
squish slimy layers of soggy leaves
and I quickly push off
into rippling green reflections of trees

The skin on my fingers
is beginning to shrivel
and as I squint
in the glare of brilliant sun
bouncing off the surface

like a turtle's
my head bobs up and down
again and again
till the shrill screech of a bird up above
short-circuits my senses
and dousing the fire
I suddenly dive
in a silent hiss of invisible steam
then slowly rise
to dangle and drift
afloat
in the welcome abyss

What She Wears

In the Costa Rican Rain Forest

Beneath a heavy canopy,
dressed in a form-fitting gown,
in endless shades of vibrant green,
mossy velvet,
miniscule leaves of satin and lace,
she stretches up
toward glittering misty slivers of sunshine
that brilliantly catch
the drops of dew
she wears as jewels

In Touch

As shadow-sounds lurk
I pull my strokes
through depths of hidden water

Alive with the moon
I *am*
my surroundings

Those fearing water snakes
won't understand
why I've sought such primal space

Untamed
unleashed
I see my reflection

The night
holds no threat
for me

Deep In The Shallows

As I glide
    through the shallows

the only sound's
the plunk-splashing slosh
of my paddle

Multi-hued dragonflies
curl into coupling,
           drifting
                over the hull
and hordes
of tiny black insects
are skating on the surface

Skittering,
         they jump,
doing the jitterbug

They radiate ripples,
      leaving ribbon-trails
          behind,
while dancing
over shadows and waves,
reflected below
on swirling
     sandy
   hillocks,
dips,
   and sunlit
  feathery
    swaying
      amber-green.

Unaware

Wellfleet, Cape Cod, MA, Summer 2012

I walk through the salt marsh
surrounded by the fiddlers'* soothing hum

What seem to be tranquil tan flats,
up close,
are scrambling with thousands of lopsided crabs,
digging tunnels
in a tuneful race against tides

but I'm in no hurry
on my path of firm wet sand
as I slowly pass through a palette of greens
in flattened swirls of salt-hay,
clumps of sea-pickles
and tall sturdy grasses, with upright off-white tassels

Telltale signs
are everywhere,
in straw-like, wave-shaped detritus
at the base of dunes
and rivulets of fast-moving water
but like tiny fish and sea creatures in microcosmic pools,
unaware of being left behind,
I'm alive,
in this changing world
of plants, sea and sand

with no sense
of time
or tides.

*fiddler crabs make a buzz-humming sound

In the Band

Under moonshine
I swim
through luminescent ripples
dappled in shadow and light

With the rhythmic swish
of breaststroke arms
and well-timed whooshes
of bubbling breaths

I'm percussion

in the band
of chirping tenor
and bullfrog bass

Choosing The River

The pool's just fine
but I take the extra steps
down to where the river bends
under the ancient erector-set bridge
and icy swirls ripple around rocks
in the shallows

Fish are flipping

The current pulls

Insects are skimming the surface

I gingerly step over stones
on my way
to be the one who dares to dive in

Then afterward,
on a high,
I break through the surface
and splashing
rise like a trout
toward earthy sweet-scented air

Having imbibed fresh water's essence
I've chosen intoxication
over what's just fine.

Where I Need to Be

Trying to reach you
on the other side
I step
from sandy shore
into deeper water

slipping and sliding
on the slimy curved surfaces
of river-smoothed rocks

Teetering
back and forth
I balance myself
with airplane arms

and dig
my curled toes
into the sand
between stones

Then anchored
standing still

I finally relax

in the calmness
of ripples
and flow

On The Right Path

We all came together
for this thirty mile ride
but I've fallen behind
on my old lady bike.
I hold my hands tight
on its high handlebars,
knowing the arthritis
in my neck
will be fine,
and I listen
as the spring
beneath my seat
squeaks,
as I sit
on this fat-ass gel-padded seat
slowly pumping
and pedaling on,
till I realize
that no one's waiting
for me.
While feeling abandoned
I notice
the pace that I keep
makes it easy to see sunlit ferns
and brilliant-green algae
afloat in the stream.

The heck with them.
I'm slowing down.

I'm right where I should be.

Queen of Weeds

With her striking *"Here I am!"* stance,
amid scruffy patches of dirt and grass
at the edges of country roads,
in ditches, abandoned fields and next to stone walls

dressed in bright form-fitting green,
with her arms outstretched
her lean body tall
and head held high,
with its lacy off-white crown

Anne's more than just a pretty weed
boasting

Keenly aware of her ancestry,
she taps into the hidden strength
of her wild-carrot roots,
to make it perfectly clear
her name is no misnomer.

Seaweed Sounds

Walking the breakwater
I notice something peeking out
from between the rocks
and bend down to pick it up,
this straggly bunch
of slippery dripping black and gold ribbon strands,
their surfaces dotted with small swollen pockets

I hold a piece of childhood
in my hands,
memories of strolling the beach
with Daddy, my sister and the dog,
skimming stones
and shells,
my toes dancing at the water's edge
digging, then wriggling
into the hard-soft sand,
the laughter of unabashed joy,
and I press my fingers hard
against the seaweed's
fluid-filled bumps,
but they're too wet,
not ready yet

I remember pressing those tiny pouches
just to hear them snap,
and suddenly
I know why
I love the touch and popping sounds
of bubble-wrap.

Need

Water and air are one with heat
as I sit by the pool breathing chlorine
while longing for lake

the raw scent of pine, soil and grass

the icy water that paints my skin in shivery bumps

and smoothes my hair into silk

the slippery fish and wild-water weeds

that graze my arms and shins

I need to swim
and never
see the bottom

Lullaby

Death Valley National Park

They come in hordes,
awed by my angles, edges, salt flats, dunes,
high canyon walls

They look beyond the grey
to see the contrast of my bright orange and aqua cliffs,
dark jagged peaks against blue sky
and rolling billows of white

They don't see that like an oversized child
I only appear to be old
and have millions of years before me
for those edges and peaks to wear down

The crust of earth, its moving plates
will rattle, crack and fold my bones,
arid hot air will blast me with sand,
flash floods dragging tons of debris
will scrape my walls and floors

but every day in the late afternoon
when the sun shifts before sunset,
it offers me blankets of dark purple shadow
whose softness unfolds
into crevices and river carved bowls,
as I welcome its soft glow of pink and gold

till cradled in the deepest of blues,
safe beneath the nightlight of moon,
I drift
into sleep
to the silent rhythmic tune
of blinking stars.

Offerings

Bearing
    the imprint
        of water
           and wind
    marsh grasses
        matted
          and swirled
offer bowls
    full of
      chartreuse
        and shadow

In The Lull

It's midsummer,
though barely seventy degrees
under a dim-misty haze of backlit grey.
The forecast is dire and everyone's gone.

I try to blend into the silence,
slowly pushing and pulling the water
and only breathing whispered breaths

The water's so still and clear
I see trout hovering weightless, waiting and watching,
schools of mirror-like minnows
flashing by tall swaying ribbons of grass,
and dark-brown leafy debris
strewn with green-tinged pebbles and rocks

Moving forward
I find a patch of orange-gold velvety powder,
a small roller-skating rink
where water-bugs gliding cut patterns

Dragonflies are hiding as if sensing something's wrong,
but in this lull before rolling black clouds
bring bolts of brilliant white,
thunderclaps, heavy rain,
and wind whips waves into a frenzy,
sucking bugs and pollen beneath the surface

The earth, the sky, the lake and I
are blissfully
in denial.

In Her Own Skin*

Inspired by the Farmington River

While sitting
    in the water
        soaking up sunshine
            she wears her nakedness
                with voluptuous grace
        and in a sideways glance
      she gazes
at her ample
stretched-out self
  with a sense of satisfaction
    in her soliid curves
        half-submerged
           in the river
              that rolls
        in ripples
      around her
and with the weight
of her body
and fleshy thighs
  she's a force of nature,
      a thriving lush island
          who decides
             how the water flows

* *This poem was also inspired by Michael Patterson's painting, Through The Water, which is the cover image for this book*

The Nature of Ecstasy

Barefoot,
I stroll with intention,
as I press my slippery steps
into the moist lushness
of early morning grass,
then suddenly stop
to stand perfectly still
and welcome the wakening wind
that stirs
the gossamer folds
of my gown
and lays its bodice
against my flesh.
I open myself
to the new day,
its incipient rays,
broad strokes
of pink-purple-orange
tinged white,
and baby blue sky.
I slowly inhale
the cool-clear scent
of last night's lingering gift,
spread my arms,
lift up my face,
hold out my palms,
and shiver
as warmth
suddenly flows
through my veins.

A Blur of Colors

From somewhere,
seemingly out of thin air,
an early summer snow-shower
of dandelion puffs
comes swirling down
around me,
dancing on invisible waves
of warmth,
blurring bright green
and the blueness of sky,
with fluffy parachutes of white,
whose delicate seeds
after drifting toward earth,
will transform themselves
slowly
into yellow.

Inner Light

Swimming
with my head above water
I slowly breathe in
the pungent sweet scent of pine
and tilt my face
towards the warmth up above

and though my eyes
are almost perfectly closed
a golden glow
sifts through

I notice
tiny weightless droplets of water
clinging to my lashes
like iridescent baubles
of Tiffany glass

Splashing
I flip
onto my back
and floating
close my eyes so tightly
the light explodes
into tiny white
       dashing
    firework flashes
that fizzling
     fall and fade
       in the dark

Awakening II

Wisps of wind
        tickle the air,
   stirring leaves
         from summer sleep,
skimming the lake,
         swaying in steam,
   softly displacing
          mosquitoes in wait,
sifting through screens,
       setting curtains aswirl,
   brushing
     soggy
        half asleep souls.
Forerunner of thunder,
       soon lightning will fly
  and rain
     will awaken the world.

Mixed Signals

My favorite wildflower
finally announces herself
in a bold celebration of summer
as her lanky bright-green stems
and saucers of lacy-white blossoms
take over

but my joy is brief

her exuberant arrival
a signal
the season's half over

and I can almost taste
the bittersweet
of her wild-carrot roots

When We Communed

My father
talked incessantly
and wore Hawaiian shirts

He engulfed
and embarrassed
us all

but when we went fishing
the rocking motions of the boat
the soil scent of baited hooks
sunshine and silence
were enough

Safety in Numbers

Living patterns
of abstract art
seemingly painted
with the broadest brush
in massive
flashing
silvery swirls
are just tiny sardines
swimming in schools

Gracefully contorting
stretching out
they twirl
by the thousands
in tornado-like tunnels
then swiftly
accordion squeeze themselves
into glistening spinning balls

huge yet elusive
morphing from moment to moment
moving from place to place
more predator than prey
they whoosh through the water
as one

No one follows or leads
There's no need

Motion Picture

Rippling reflections
      flash
           from the stream,
projecting
      motion,
          translucent sun-shadows,
flickering glitter
        on trees

The Air Show

Thousands
      of swallows
          flying
             as one
   are changing color
shape
      wings opening
  closing
      black to white
in perfect rhythm
         catching wind
    Venetian blinds*
         in flight

*A window covering made of metal slats that are similar
to, but wider than, today's mini-blinds

For Winter

The sweet metallic taste of lake
mingles with scent of pine

The warmth of sun bakes my skin
till droplets disappear into sky
where the view
is clear unobstructed blue

Touching sand
with my toes,
smiling,
I sigh,
close my eyes,
as deep in the moment
of summer,
I hold onto it
tightly
for winter.

Winter's Hint

It's calling

a distant reminder
I've probably had my last swim

as a honk-flapping black irregular V
                              rushes over my head
in its ominous cool backdrop of grey

before
        leaves
                    turn
                        yellow
                              orange
                                    red
            fall down
                        turn brown
        and crumble
beneath
a wintery burden
of white.

Beyond Bare Branches

"No spring nor summer beauty hath such grace, as
I have seen in one autumnal face."

~ John Donne

"Pleasure lies thickest where no pleasures seen:
There's not a leaf that falls upon the ground but
holds one joy of silence or sound..."

~ Laman Blanchard

Autumn Marsh

Salt marsh straws
        sucked dry of green
    are matted down
                like scruffy hair
    cowlick spiked
                unruly drab
        against the earth's
                    broad scalp

Beavers at Bantam

Dragging our kayaks into the water,
we search for just the right time
at the edge of dusk or dawn

It's hit or miss

but it's worth trudging over the dams
just to have them surround me,
swimming with such purpose,
beady eyes
    and big black noses
           pressing forward
till suddenly
they realize
we're there

What's magic to me
may be mundane
       but the loud smack-slapping sound
   of their broad flat tails
propelling them
           down
makes the hairs
at the nape of my neck
stand on end.

Assault

Raindrops
        suspended
from rails
    on the deck
sway,
  as scrub pines
      slow dance
to the pulse
of crooning
salt wind,
till the hurricane,
      swallowing calm,
slapping ashore
spews its rain,
forcing wind-songs
      into howls,
snapping elastic trees,
speeding
the domino fall
of marsh reeds and grasses,
slicing air
    with dune-stolen sand.

Finding Her Way

This goose
has flown far
from her arrowhead flock

While flapping her wings of grey
she's abandoned all black and white
and swerving
carves a confident path
in a current
she claims as her own

Keeping perfect time isn't her style
She's left the rhythm behind

but when the other geese land
in the field by the stream
she'll be already feasting
on sedge

Passing Us By

Today
though it's just the beginning
of autumn

as a flash
of red-yellow-orange
bursts from the lushness of green

I know
that in an instant
all the colors
will be gone

that the whiteness
of ice and snow
will take over

then suddenly fall
from branches
soon full
of blossoming buds

and the multi-hued palette
of summer
like a child's top
with colors blurred

will spin
wobble
then tumble

toward the dark

Transition

The soft underbellies
    of purple-grey clouds
        scattered across
          a fading blue sky
            are awash
       in the luminous blush
     of leftover sunlight
   easing itself
into dusk

River Rodeo

Riding
        on riffles
and bucked
            by waves,
reflections
            of trees
                    and sky
rise
    and
        fall
slapping
        into
            stone saddles

Enjoying the Leftovers

The Farmington River, just below the dam in Collinsville, CT

After the water has fallen,
delicate bubbles
flowing downstream
have a drama all their own
as they sparkle
off-white
reflecting the sun
　and gather together
　　　　　in patches of foam
　　　　　　　　that bumping
　　　　　and bobbing
　　ride over riffles
　and slide
　　around rocks
　　　　　in their way

Water Song II

Air pushes
    and pulls
  the lake's surface
      to the sounds
of a lapping beat
    stretching and squeezing
  clouds and trees
      into accordion folds

Haunted

Lake McDonough, Barkhamsted , CT*

I lean back to gaze up
at grey overstuffed clouds,
backlit and rimmed in white against blue,
then slowly
         pulling my paddle
I listen
    to the tinkling
         of tiny waves
                  tapping
              and splashing
                  the hull
                     of my boat
as a turtle's shiny brown head

                              pops out
but I'm aware
that down deep
there are waterlogged ghosts
watching fishes
                  swim up
                and down
                     soggy hills,
into liquid valleys,
            across sodden fields,
in between foundations
                  of churches, general stores and houses,
as their whispered wishes
                     float to the surface,
telling me
         what I wish
                  I didn't know.

**The town of Barkhamsted Hollow was buried in the process of creating this
reservoir that supplies water to Greater Hartford*

Late September

Peach and gold
       on tiptoes of red
           prance
               across the treetops
Making merry
    the dance of death
they bring joy
        to fading green
aglow
    in a gilded
           crimson
               finale
November's bare branches
unseen

Daylight Savings

There's an aura
in the silence
of mingled shadow and light
as slowly the day switches over
and in sadness I sit at the dining room table
looking inside and out
through confusion
toward the warm glow that wafts
from the top of the stairs
and the rouge-tinted blanket
of leftover fading blue sky
beyond the bay window
as darkness takes over late afternoon
in this room
full of unwelcome evening

Caught In A Sideways Glance

Spider web sparkling
in the early morning sun,
bejeweled
in translucent pearls,
droplets of glistening dew,
strung together
on shimmering strands
of silk

Pause

My heels slam the hard Carolina sand
as cirrus-streaked sky
rests on silty green sea

Soothed by the gentlest of roars
I slow to a stop,
suck in the ocean's salty-raw scent,
while dark grey pelicans
out in the deep,
with arrows for beaks,
pouches flapping,
feathers pressed tight,
in perfect precision,
swiftly plunge
to puncture fish
beneath
the water-skin slick.

A Hint

It's mid-autumn
late afternoon
in the marsh
as bright-orange
yellow and red
flicker in the distance
against a background
of bare brittle beige
and the air
interwoven
with scent and sound
wraps us
in pungent pine
the rancid sweetness
of fermentation
wafting from emerald green pools
the rustle and crunch
of dry leaves and grass
and the background buzzing hum
clicks and chirps
of bugs and birds
as the sinking sun
spreads out
the last of its brilliant white-gold
behind a tall stand of reeds
and with trickery
transforms their overlapped fringe
into glistening illusions
of translucent ice-covered lace
hauntingly hinting
of winter

Autumn Morning

The chill
of morning mist
at first
     floats thickly
    on the lake
slowly unfurling
      its foggy self
onto shadowed reflections
        of fiery hills
flowing opaque
to translucent
as rising up
it invisibly blends
        into blue

Autumn Eve's Chill

Gusting
      from nowhere
winter's hint
   ripples the surface
        of silence

In a split-second race
  leftover light
      sails
        on a shiver
          of waves

Last of the Leaves

In a final performance,
autumnal red and gold confetti
                          flies from trees
but this time
there's no encore.

As sun
        surreptitiously
   steals away
wind will be whistling
through empty trees

and fallen leaves
will slowly turn to dust.

Beyond Bare Branches I and II

I

I've shed my frilly colorful clothes,
am back to basic brown,
and with the gawkers gone
I thrive
in the quiet transition of seasons

Finally able to see,
I breathe freely,
deeply
under wide-open sky,
as reaching out
I welcome the sunshine
that flows
into my roots and core
with warmth for winter.

II

Though she held on for weeks,
her vivid patchwork quilt
still slid to the ground,
and now she stands naked
slender and tall,
learning to love
being exposed

She gracefully stretches her arms
and with fluttering fingers
beckons the breeze
to touch her bare skin,
as she stands in the fullness of sunshine,
her branches and trunk
soaking it in,
and waits
to be covered in white.

On the Cusp

High in the saddle,
gently jolted
back and forth,
my legs pressed
against the warm solid curve
of flexing muscled haunches,
one hand wrapped
in the soft loop of well-fingered reins,
the other holding the leather-smooth horn,
up and down,
forward I ride
to the clop-clatter and heavy thud
of hooves
on pine needle padding
and coarsely crushed rock,
past fields
full of crisp beige stalks
of leftover corn,
through autumnal tunnels of plants and trees.
burnt orange, evergreen, crimson, gold, peach,
faded yellow-beige ferns,
their crisp brown edges curled,
and I breathe in the clear sap-scented air,
as spinning
unhinged leaves
drift towards earth,
in the prescience
of a rustling cool breeze.

Late Autumn Truth

Caught in the gap
between leaves and snow
stripped of softness
skeletal trees
scratch ghosts
onto slate blue sky

In Between

I no longer grieve
for the lushness of green
or the brilliance
of orange
yellow
and red

I've found
a new perspective

exposed
    between naked trees

I take in the sight
    of powder-puffed
        grey and beige hills
     rolling
       towards stubbled
           golden-brown fields

and see lacy patterns
       in the delicate bones
   of overlapped branches
           against
             azure blue
     in the unadorned view
   between seasons

Winterlude

"In winter you feel the bone structure of the
landscape."
~ Andrew Wyeth

"I please myself with the graces of the winter
scenery, and believe that we are as much touched by
it as by the genial influences of summer."
~ Ralph Waldo Emerson

Holiday Decorations

In celebration

the storm
sprinkles mirrors
on the world

Pine cones
become ornaments
draped
in glassy strands

No foil strips
of imitation ice

Glitter and tinsel
are real

No rhythmic patterns
of colored lights

Sun and shadow
are taking turns

Back To Earth

Stand quietly
    Listen
  The tinkling of snow
       is tapping on oak leaves
            of autumn's neglect
      The weight will unhinge them
              to finally fall
                 into waves of cold
      as paper-thin feathers of crisp faded brown
slowly swirling and swaying
    till softly
        they rest
           on a bed of fresh flakes
             beneath gathering layers
                 of white

Longings

My husband insists
he wants to go South,
but I want to stay
real,
aware of the seasons
passing me by

Though I fully inhabit
each warm floral moment,
it's contrast
that makes them stand out

so who needs Paradise
with its heavenly essence of death?

Falling leaves
open hidden views,
and bare gnarled branches
have a beauty of their own,
as does snow,
whose glorious white
is a momentary fantasy
punctuating truth
as it melts.
It's the wind-whipped cold,
numbing fingers
and stinging cheeks,
that awakens the soul
to notice budding hints
of what's to come,
feeding dreams
of summer
and the longings
that keep me alive.

Control

Watching the river
                from a window,
        my mind
                drifts off
                        to the constant flow
                of water and ice,
        beneath banks of snow

till I suddenly notice
all motion
has stopped,

that pieces of ice
have gathered together

filling in gaps,
to complete a puzzle,
that hadn't existed before

I stare at them,
pressed tightly together,
yet separate

and as if they've partied too long,
            are done with casual conversation,
                they begin to break apart,
        to go their own separate ways,
but they're really controlled
                    by the current
                imperceptibly
        pushing them on.

Stolen Glory

Glittering icicle trees
shedding their crystalline cloaks
are cackling
crying
bending
and brooding
as sunshine
steals glory away

Under The Surface

Roaring Brook, Canton, CT

Suspended motion
        crackled in ice
glitters
    on the stream
Bubbles
     pressed up
        against canopy glass
zigzagging,
      gurgle through snares
till finally
     water
       spills out
         over stones
splashing freedom
      on snow-covered banks

Seduction

There's flirtation
in the intermittent swoops and swirls
of falling flakes
outside my window,
as the day stands still,
and winter begins to seduce me
beneath its gathering sheets
of white,
filling me first
with the softness of silence,
then a guilty sense
of giddy play,
and in a momentary fantasy
of whitewashed sins,
I forgive the stinging bite of wind
and the frightening touch
of hidden ice.

Asana*

It's that cabin fever
time of year

Needing more
than a treadmill
facing a wall,
I take myself
to the trail
to walk
among hints of history,
surround myself
with the soothing-shrill echo
of train whistle memories

I stick out my tongue
to taste snowflakes
as others melt in my hair

People with iPods
pass me by
but I'm tuned
into the past,
earth and sky,
the rustling
of hungry hawks
in trees,
the sound
of scrunching snow.

My mind's
in a yoga pose.

*means pose in Sanskrit

Right Side Up

With a slip-sliding thud
I'm suddenly flat on my back
legs stuck straight up
poles poking blue sky
but I'm more than all-right

My criss-crossed skis
are framing slow-motion clouds
and everything else also slows down
as smiling
I lie
on this bed
of soft white

The rest of the trail
and hot cider
can wait

I'm savoring the view
upside down

Winter's Trail

On snowshoes
in stillness
I stand afloat

watching snow
gently drift from trees

gazing ahead
at the bold stripe
of trail
deep
in powdery white

Though distant
and dulled
the trickling tones
of river
under cover of ice
seep beneath my earmuffs

To these mantras
of sound and sight
I begin my hike

having
already
arrived

Last Licks

She
     drops
          a few inches
of snow

yet we know
she still has to choose
to move from winter
to spring

but unwilling,
full of bluster

she batters
the hopeful
with wind.

Saving The Seasons

"We do not inherit the earth from our ancestors.
We borrow it from our children."

~ Chief Seattle

"We are members of one great body, planted by
nature. ... We must consider that we were born for
the good of the whole."

~ Seneca

The following poems are about our environment. They were birthed quite differently from many of the other poems in this book. Instead of being in a peaceful meditative state when I wrote them, there was a cacophonous interference in my mind as I found myself wondering what future we will be leaving to our children. Up until the last poem, my message is a grim one. We need to listen to the wisdom of Native Americans and others who truly have a healthy vision and respect for the earth we all share. It's not too late to save our precious planet and so I have chosen to end this book with a hopeful poem about some of the positive actions that are already being taken.

Accidental Environmentalist

Inspired by the Albert Bierstadt painting "In The Mountains"(1867)

His painting
glows
from within

its pieces pulled
from different places

an idealized location

The lake reflects trees
blue sky
clouds
The mountains and cliffs
soar
above tumbling waterfalls

A pervasive mist
conjures silence
and awe

as if Bierstadt
intensified it all
to remind us today
that tomorrow
it might be gone

Silenced

In the lushness of jungle
this small black and yellow bird*
anxiously skitters
back and forth on a branch

He's once again singing
his half of a love song
as bobbling
he points his beak
and longingly
stretches out his neck

only now
when he trills
it's to an empty tree
and though he waits
each time
before warbling again
there'll never be a she
to answer him back
no nest to be made
no eggs will be hatched

He's about to succumb
to a broken heart
and ours
will be filled
with the silence

*The O'o bird was a species that lived on the Hawaiian island of Kaua'i and
has recently become extinct. The last bird of its kind was recorded singing, and it
can be seen and heard in the film Racing To Extinction. The extinction of our
world's species continues at an alarming rate.*

The New View

from my tiny tumbled rock beach
is of smooth river stones,
spongy emerald moss,
on boulders of slippery grey,
sumac,
maples,
oak branches
bowing down
at the edge

The river
bends
under an old narrow bridge
of rusting beige-painted struts

There are dense
endless
variations on green,
rippling shades
of brown

and as fish flip
and twirl themselves,
while dancing free

I suddenly notice
construction signs and bright orange stripes
sprayed on trees.

Encounter

Avon Mountain, Route 44, Avon, CT, Spring 2000*

As the wild lose their wilderness
and wander into backyards
I learn to hide trash-cans
while calmly accepting the presence of bears

until I meet one
in the middle of the road
and see its magnitude
up close.

For a dangerous moment
our eyes meet

then fumbling in seeming slow-motion
I try to swerve out of the way
But it's too late
and its hindquarters
graze the front end

In this clash of two worlds
mud splatters from fur onto fenders

and my nostrils are seared
by putrid musky pungent fumes
pushing through cracks
in windows and doors

as I wonder
which one of us
belongs

* *Not long ago, it was highly unusual to spot bears or other wildlife in Connecticut. It has become commonplace in the 21st century.*

Ostriches

West of center
the hills and whole neighborhoods
are enveloped in flames
while in the middle of the country
farmers are forced to cut and clear fields
full of bean-less soy and stunted stalks of cob-less corn

Further West
the mighty Colorado is shrinking
as ranchers run out of grasslands for cattle to graze

There are too many straws in the river
and manmade Lake Meade is being sucked dry

Soon San Diego, like its neighbor Tijuana,
will show its true shades of tan

and in yet another hottest of summers
an invisible toxic shroud hovers over the land

Prices of food will soon rise
yet ads on TV are touting coal

Those ads are paid for by people like those
who cracked Ohio's earth open
with their euphemistic fracking,
subterranean shatterings,
in search of unnatural gas

Greed trumps the future
as they stick their heads
in the same dusty sand
that is destined
to cover us all.

Power Outage

Waters
>> gush
>>>> over
>>>>>> tribal lands
White man
>>>> has turned on
>>>>>>>> the faucet
While power
>>>> flows
>>>>>> from Hydro-Quebec*
the power
>>>> of wilderness
>>>>>>>> drowns

*The James Bay power stations represent almost half of Hydro-Québec's total output and capacity. There was acrimonious conflict with the 5,000 Crees of Northern Quebec over land rights, lifestyle, and environmental issues.
The James Bay Project required the diversion of several rivers and the creation of large reservoirs that greatly altered the environment. Hydro-Quebec is one of the largest water projects in the world.

Power

The windmills of the San Gorgonio Pass Wind Farms in Palm Springs, CA

In celebration
giants stand
tall and proud
gathered together
in endless rows
atop jagged stone mountains
and on the dusty scrub-covered
valley floor

Slowly
steadily
they whirl their arms
in a rhythmic ritual
sinuous dance
overlapping hundreds of hands
to the hum
of the turbines' chant

As wind transforms
and current invisibly flows

the tribal reverence
for earth
is finally heard

About the Author

Award-winning poet Joan Kantor lives with her husband in the charming village of Collinsville, Connecticut. Joan's training is in education as well as marriage and family therapy, and she was a college counselor and Learning Disabilities Specialist for many years. She actively promotes poetry in the community and is a member of the International Academy for Poetry Therapy. She has been a featured reader for the public television series *Speaking of Poetry* as well as for several art museums; additionally, she leads workshops, has mentored for Poetry Out Loud, and judged and mentored for the Hill-Stead Museum's Sunken Garden Poetry Festival Fresh Voices Poetry Program. To fulfill her inclusive vision of the arts, Joan collaborates with both visual artists and musicians and currently performs in *Stringing Words Together*, an interactive program of poetry and violin music.

Kantor's first published collection, *Shadow Sounds*, was a finalist for the *Foreword Reviews* Book of the Year Award in 2010. Her poetry has also been included in numerous literary journals, in 2013, she won first prize in The Hackney Literary Awards poetry contest and in 2015 she took First Place for Poetry for her book *Fading Into Focus*, in the Writer's Digest 23rd Annual Self-Published Book Awards. Her book, *Too Close For Comfort*, will be published by Aldrich Press in 2016.

www.joankantorpoetry.com

Made in the USA
Middletown, DE
29 March 2017